Give Yourself A Pay Rise

Jack Briggs

Table of Contents

INTRODUCTION

CHAPTER 1

THERE'S TROUBLE PERCOLATING UNDER YOUR NOSES: THE COFFEE PROBLEM

CHAPTER 2

SWITCH UTILITIES: WHY THE INERTIA TO SWITCH PROVIDERS?

CHAPTER 3

PACKING A SAVINGS PUNCH WITH PACKED LUNCHES

CHAPTER 4

CASHING IN ON CASHBACK POINTS MAKE YOUR MONEY WORK FOR YOU!!

CHAPTER 5

GETTING CAUTIOUS WITH CASHBACK WEBSITES

CHAPTER 6

CLEANING UP THE DIRECT DEBIT CLOSET

CHAPTER 7

HANDLING DEBT INTERESTS LIKE A PRO

Introduction

Don't wait for it! They aren't going to give to you! The only way you'll get that pay rise that you so badly want, deserve and yearn for is by taking action. The fact is, it probably won't come and if it does, it will be something closer to a 2% cost of living increase, which based on the UK average salary of £27,500 would be £550 and after the tax man has had his fucking poisonous slice that totals a whopping £374. Don't get me wrong this is not to be dismissed but what could you really do with that £31 a month? Get a gym membership that you'd never go to? Go to the cinema? Not with £31! What about that impulse purchase that you don't really need or afford but your hand is magnetised to pick it up or click on add to cart. The answer to the original question is fuck all, but what if you had 3 x that a month? 6x? 10x?

This book is only the foundation of what will become your money making/money saving mindset that will multiply your income and net worth. But all I can do is show you how once you finish each chapter; it will be down to you to take action. Don't think anyone else is going to help you with this; it's down to YOU! AS you turn every page and complete every chapter, you will become more aware of what's always been around you. Is this book the passage to financial freedom? No, no it's not but it's my experience that rarely exists although the idea is sold throughout the world either in forex trading, real estate investment and many other ways. With this idea, you can sign up to a 3-day course and you'll have all the skills you need to become a millionaire. Take this from me and I've researched a lot of highly successful people and none of them started with the immortal lines "I went to a seminar and took a 3-day course". But at the end disappointingly, 95% of the people reading this won't follow the advice of this book, you'll read the content and be amazed that you have never thought of the techniques in this book nor have you done the SIMPLE maths that will allow you to generate those extra zero's in your bank account without relying on anyone. All you need to do is to carry out some basic alterations to your mindset on how you spend your hard earned cash and you will give yourself a pay rise.

Chapter 1

There's Trouble Percolating under Your Noses: The Coffee Problem

Across the globe, people always think of us Britons as avid tea lovers with posh accents and awful teeth. If you ever go to Barnsley, you'll find that that's not the case about the tea now-a-days. Gone are the days when Cutty Sark brought over some of the finest Oolong and other fragrant teas from the Orient. It has statistically been proven that tea is in danger of being a dismal drink that was once everyone's favourite, because there's a new favourite in town or in the country. It's that gorgeous rich, silky addictive kick start that you need every morning, that's right kids you guessed it's our old friend Carlito Coffee! (everything gets a name). People across almost all age groups are now increasingly drinking more and more cups of coffee than tea. In fact, here are some interesting numbers to give you an idea of how much coffee exactly we are talking about here.

- It has been found that Britons who stay away from home consumed 2.1 billion cups of coffee, while just 874 million cups of tea were consumed in the same year. These numbers are as per a report that was released in the year 2015, so the numbers are bound to have shot up since then. More joy for Costa!

- The rise in the trend for the love of coffee has been on the upswing since the early noughties, when there were coffee shop chains established by the big brands – Starbucks, Costa, Café Nero. Whoever your brand of choice is, several other brands and chains have been set-up to give it a stiff competition

- Are we talking about plain old cups of coffee here? Nescafe original milk and sugar? Or just a regular filter coffee? No, that just doesn't seem to sit well with most of us these days. We tend to lean more towards the speciality coffees such as cappuccino or latte or for that extra treat cameral latte with extra sauce and cream., which could cost around £4 a cup.

- There were approximately 486 million cups of cappuccinos sold in 2015, while 431 million cups of Americanos occupied the second spot in terms of sales. These saw a respective rise of 12% and 33% since 2012.

- The UK is behind just two European countries in terms of consumption. The top spot is held by Italy with 4.78 billion cups per annum, while the second spot has been snagged by France, at 2.27 billion cups. The UK is followed by Germany and Spain respectively.

- An important thing to note about coffee consumption in the UK is that it is the only country which reported a rise in the trend in the past five years, especially by people who stay away from home.

So, you're probably like yes great I like coffee we all do what's the problem? Notice the types of coffees that have been listed in the above facts' list? They all talk about speciality coffees that you tend to drink in cafes and restaurants and don't make at home. In fact, there has been a significant drop in the traditionally brewed coffee market, while coffee chains have seen a growth in their profits in the UK and some of them don't pay their fair share in tax but that's something for another day. These specialized coffees aren't cheap, especially if you don't have enough money to cover the other important expenses in your life. (that's where you fill in the blanks). Let's look at it a little deeper.

Human beings put their problems into the back of their mind, so they don't have to deal with them. If an issue can be avoided, it will be until it gets so out of hand that it must be dealt with, then you get a pay day loan (but that's the last chapter). So, when you are driving or walking to work and that small voice that whispers "large latte and almond croissant" Don't give in to it; it's easier said than done, isn't it? Well, what if you already had your fix before leaving the house? Although, these drinks and pastries are meant to be a treat, you had one yesterday, the day before that and every single day last week. So, it's no longer a treat; it's now every necessity that you have brought into your life so it probably doesn't taste as good as it did when you had one for a treat, so you are actually doing yourself an injustice by doing this every day. You are depriving yourself of what you had before. So, what do we do?

The other bad habit we have is to avoid guilt by trying to find ways to fool ourselves. We go to a coffee shop and we spend a small amount one day, that voice is back and tells you – it's such a small amount, so its fine its £4.34, you work your fingers to the bone only to spend it on coffee grounds, water and milk and for what, you have it that much that you don't even get the enjoyment of the taste anymore. But its ok you've paid by contactless, so you don't even see the money leaving your account. So, the feeling of guilt is a little lesser than what we would have felt had colourfully printed paper and shiny coins gone from our hands. The small amount that we spend on one cup turns out to be a pretty big deal at the end of the year. If we were to add up the number of cups we drank during the year. Just think about the number of times you've been guilty of doing this yourself (and you must be honest when you do so!), and you'll know what I'm talking about.

Here are some more important numbers.

- Worldwide, about 2 billion cups of coffee are consumed every single day. In the UK alone, roughly 55 million cups are consumed per day, and a significant number of people prefer drinking flavoured or fancy coffees.

- Out of the people who frequent coffee shops, at least 80% do so on a weekly basis, while roughly 16% visit them on a daily basis. The latter is the statistic that you do not want to fall into.

Consider yourself to be a person who visits coffee shops on a daily basis, and you prefer a traditional cup of cappuccino mostly. I've not seen many people opting for a small cup because we usually tend to think that by adding just a little more to the bill, we get a decent sized cup of coffee so that the flavour can actually be savoured. When you come to check out you hear;

Barista: Would you like any pastries with that?

Stomach: Course I fucking would I want the whole fucking shelf!!

Mind: But they're nearly 3 squids each and do you really need one you've only come in for a coffee!

Mouth: Yes, I'll have an Almond Croissant please.

Sound familiar?

Giving up on a habit that is akin to food of the gods is not easy, is it? People indeed face a lot of struggle to do well at work or in social circles, so enjoying good food and drinks is certainly not something you should give up on. We're talking about giving yourself a pay rise and not become a social recluse. If your friends ring you and ask to go for coffee, then go for it! You don't have to give this up completely. You could instead do things which give you what you desire but in a smart and efficient way so you don't spend a load of money on something that's gone within 5 minutes. Think efficiency and economy, think being able to savour the delights of different types of coffee right at home, be your own barista and you could still make a habit of drinking your favourite brew without going broke. The solution is simple if you haven't worked it out already – make coffee at home!

A visit to Starbucks or Costa need not just result in a single cup of coffee and a slice of cake that you consume and easily forget about. You could buy instant and I'm not talking about shitty freeze-dried shit I'm talking about good barista style coffee. What about making a onetime investment on a good bean to cup coffee machine or hob top percolator. There are several models of coffee machines that are easily available online or in your nearest in most supermarkets today, which you can easily operate.

So, let's run the numbers and show you what your spending and what you're going to start saving.

Large Cappuccino & Almond Croissant = £4.34

x 5 days a week = £21.17

x 4 weeks = £84.68

x 12 months in a year = £1,100.84

x 5 years = £5504.20

Look for the alternatives, most coffee companies now even do barista style instant coffee. I use personally I use Nescafe Crema, its good and probably one of the more expensive instants but it's definitely worth it. A packet of Crema costs roughly £7.00 this would get you 111 servings. Works out about 6 pence a cup. The whole jar would easily last you about a month, for a family, if you are a moderate coffee drinker. Those who are currently caffeine junkies – advice is you quit drinking so much coffee firstly, and reduce your dependency on it! Then, you could start drinking 2-3 cups of coffee per day, like a normal human being!

Those who have never given instant coffee a shot or had a cup of it about a year back and have forgotten what it tastes like – get yourself a decent cup of instant coffee today. For all you know, you'll give up on those fancy flavoured coffees and stick to the more traditional instant or black coffees, thereby saving you a lot more money and efforts in making your favourite brew.

Do the maths, run the numbers it's a double positive – you are saving hundreds of pounds and giving your intestines a break from fatty snacks! There are other co-related costs that you could be saving o, such as the cost of treating someone else to a cup of coffee because you don't like visiting a coffee shop alone, the cost of travelling to and from a coffee shop, any tips that you may leave, and any merchandise you are tempted to buy from that shop on the way to your favourite store that you visit. Plus, an added benefit of having coffee making equipment and ingredients at home is that you can have the drink any time of the day, without any hassle! Late night meetings, cosy afternoon showers spent with your partner, early morning kick-start machine – you name it and you would have gifted it to yourself with one simple, smart move.

You could roughly save more than 98.55% of your expenses on coffee and snacks by adopting the method of making some at home, and these savings over a number of years do add up to a big number. So get online and find a reasonably priced, long-lasting coffee making machine, or stock up on some instant coffee powder and just get fresh milk at home every day to save money yet enjoy coffee.

So, that 5 grand you spent at the start of this chapter, has now just been replaced with a forgiving £82.00. What are you waiting for? all it needs is for you to take action.

Chapter 2

Switch Utilities: Why the inertia to switch providers?

We all hate change, but we don't realize the fact that some changes in life are fucking excellent! And do you know what changes are best ones that increase those readies in your bank account? I am of course talking about changing our service and insurance providers. We, customers, are constantly being advised to switch our utility providers, but most of us tend to resist. Why? What are the barriers that stop us from doing this?

We stay with our banks longer than our beloved partners. Four-fifths of the Brits are just not bothered to look for cheaper service providers for electricity or gas despite several consumer gurus Jack Briggs included constantly urging to switch. Can you believe that 80%, I hear more than 80% of people moan about the price of energy and insurance maybe if they'd shop around the wouldn't be so pissed off about it. We choose to pay hundreds of pounds extra every year that could be spent on so many other things. Why? I'll tell you why because you can't be bothered to type in the numbers to comparison websites. Even though the process takes roughly 15 minutes from the start of the search to the finish of the switch. To be fair I can see why you'd rather spend the fifteen minutes browsing through Facebook looking at people's photos that you don't really like or care about. It takes just 15 minutes what could you do in 15 minutes? Hold that thought you saucy little sausage. Now think about what you could do with £1300 additional a year? I'll tell you Venice, Amsterdam, Rome, Paris or save it for a few years and take the kids to Disneyland, imagine the look on their faces, now think about how you're going to spend the next 15 minutes? If you have just thrown this book down to switch things over then well done to you, you have shown initiative. If you haven't then I implore you to finish this chapter then immediately before doing anything else put the book down, take your finances and make shit happen. Think about that for a second and when you turn the last page get up, go and make a change. The fact is you spend more time shopping for a toaster than you do for energy and its far simpler and a toaster doesn't save you money. Just think about that for a second you spend more time shopping for a £20 toaster than you do your £2000 energy bill. But why? Is it the laziness or we are just apathetic about getting a better deal? As per energy regulator Ofgem, it was found in a survey that 4 out of 5 of us fail to shop around for electricity and gas, costing an extra 100 pounds a year. In this case, it always better to be the 1 out of 5.

So, why are consumers so reluctant to find themselves better service providers when they love shopping around for the cheapest deal on flights or holidays? One of the possible reasons could be that they are suspicious of firms who just try to lure them away from their providers, while for others it is simply a lot of hassle thinking about finding a better alternative. Well to put your fears at bay no matter who you go with your lights well shine just as bright and your gas will keep you just as toasty with any of the energy providers. And hassle? Really? Punching a couple of numbers into your phone for 15 minutes, just think of it like playing Candy Crush!

When I moved into my first home, just off the back of a huge renovation at the time it was just easier to go with the utilities that were already set up as in my naivety I assumed that the energy companies were honest people. In reality, I couldn't have been more wrong I started out paying £110 a month gas and electric and £75 water bill within two years I was paying upwards of £180 for gas and electricity and my usage hadn't increased at all. When they got in contact, they were going to increase my direct debit. Further, I decided to move utilities and get a water meter, so I was only charged what I used. I now pay £95 per month gas and electricity and £25 per month for water. Saving me £1620 per year which over a 5-year period gives me £8100. Now I shop around every 12 months from start to finish it takes me no longer than an hour.

Looking at the figures, wouldn't you want to switch utilities? How? Well, the answer is

Uswitch, there others out there but I have found this one to not only showcase the best deals but also find it very easy to use. It is an online comparison and switching platform that helps people to compare prices and quality on a range of products and services. Uswitch can help you save money on banking services, gas and electricity, phone, insurance and finance products. The main aim is to reap the benefits of the best service and prices from suppliers. So, don't let me stop you at utilities, change everything to give yourself a fresh financial start!

How does it work? Well, uSwitch has an agreement in place with several suppliers dealing in electricity and gas, phone, finance, insurance services. They charge them an amount when they switch customers to them and offer free service to the consumers. Their commercial relationship makes the switching process as simple as possible and in certain cases, they can even get you some of the exclusive deals that are not provided by the suppliers directly.

Don't panic about your data its completely safe as the data used by uSwitch to compare suppliers and come up with the best options for you, is provided directly by the suppliers. They continuously monitor all their suppliers and update their site to ensure their results are up-to-date and comprehensive. Even for their financial services, the data they use to calculate the results are fed in directly by the suppliers.

So, there you are it will take less time to switch than It will to scroll through Facebook for 16 minutes, cook a 16-minute microwave meal and to……. For 16 minutes use your imagination #saucysausage so what are you waiting for kids. Go! Do it now save some money but make sure you do this every year as the crafty little swine's that energy providers are they will slowly creep your energy up and up until it was back where it was originally. Switching suppliers is easy to do and saves you hundreds of pounds. Stop the excuses and start switching!!

Chapter 3

Packing a Savings Punch with Packed Lunches

Back when I was constantly skint way before I installed the principles of *Give Yourself A Pay Rise* into my life I used to look at people with packed lunches and my first thought was you look ridiculous and my second thought was I have not got the time for that. How wrong was I and since I have started prepping and using what I've got at home I've started to see the benefit not only in my pocket but in energy levels, my concentration, my health and my waistline. If you eat out every day just think about how much shit you shovel in your mouth every day as most of the people manufacturing that garbage are only interested in one thing and it's not your health it's your money. When you finish this chapter, you will have one thing in common with these people and it's that you will also be interested in your money, not just interested but obsessed sa bi product of this, is that your health with also improve. So that means a win, win for us. If you monitor the cost of the lunches and dinners you have to eat outside or get delivered to your place; you may end up feeling sorrier for yourself than a duck that just swam up to someone at the pond on a low carb diet. There is definitely nothing to be ashamed of when it comes to eating home cooked and packed food; this is, in fact, a habit that one should follow obsessively to save a lot of money and increase your lifespan. So now you know you're aware of the benefits let me show you how to do this.

Apart from toddlers and retired people, most of us are either working or studying, which means we are out of our homes for at least 5 days a week, almost through the day. And don't let the word "students" fool you, ladies and gentlemen. The rigorous education system being adopted by countries all over the world requires students to be immersed in studies for at least 7 hours followed by 3-4 extra-curricular activities, internships, group studies, attending seminars and workshops, and so many other things. And there's no need to talk about the work pressures we face in almost every organization now-a-days, is there? We are forced to see how quickly the other person is moving up and down the professional hierarchy and find ways to beat the others at their own game, so we earn more and tire ourselves out faster. Extended work hours, being a part of work-related programs and outdoor activities, juggling that second job if you had to take on up – all of this can be extremely physically and emotionally draining. Now imagine if you used all the tools in this book you wouldn't have to compete for that pay rise and you wouldn't need to work that second job.

So, what does this all mean – this round the clock busy schedule that we all keep? Well, two things amongst many others. First – fuel, fuel, fuel; we need a lot of fuel to keep ourselves moving. And I don't mean the dead, fossil type sucked up by our vehicles in the blink of an eye. I'm talking about nourishment that we need to eat on a regular basis to keep your mind and body going. Food and drinks at periodic intervals are as important as dating and earning money guys. No, hang on, correction – it's *more* important than these two activities! Second – we are all pressed for time. We don't seem to find enough time to sleep a good night's sleep, rest our minds enough so we can think creatively and productively. We are so accustomed to getting by on the bare minimum rest and recreation time that we get scared of the day when we are going to retire and will have nothing else to do on our hands. Come on! Do you see the irony?! We all earn enough money, so we lead a good standard of living, but we forget what those standards imply and forget to enrich our bodies and lives with the basic things they require. You need to eat healthy food regularly to keep yourself physically fit, and you need to rest and you need to enjoy yourself to say you really lead a rich life.

So, coming back to our point of discussion – food! We know food is important, we just don't give it the importance required. A bag of crisps, some snack with a greasy, spicy sauce – most kids think when they're able to eat such things without adult supervision with their own money, they've attained adulthood. A pretty sorry state of affairs, guys. Both in terms of the deterioration of the logical thinking process of the human race and the amount of money spent on poor food. Those of you looking at your screen and smirking thinking you visit only the swanky restaurants with food names long enough to eat up a lot of paper, but food portions small enough to be missed by the eye – here's a newsflash for you. No food is as good and healthy as home-cooked food. The food that you eat outside is mostly made to titillate your taste buds so you keep having more and more of it; the primary focus of the restaurant is to make a profit and not see you participate in the next marathon or live to your 100. So, what happens is you spend a lot of money on cheesy, saucy, oil-rich food, and you burn a hole in your intestines as well as your pocket. The food eating habits of most of the youth and middle-aged people all around the world really is shocking.

Let's try and understand how changing food habits can lead you to give yourself a pay raise that you don't have to fight or compete for.

Eating out is a worrisome habit, all right. Your mom may be guilty in enjoying her plate of pasta with a glass of wine 3 days a week, but she'll secretly be remembering the times her mother drummed into her to eat her beans and grains at home in her younger days.

Sadly, not many youths who will grow up to become adults will hear such ringing voices even in their conscience because even the adults are slowly moving away from traditional home cooked food to packed food on an increased basis. So, this means that eateries will make a lot of money, but the general health and wealth of the population of the nation will be pretty low. Plus, we're talking about a lot of health issues.

The amount of money spent on eating out will be closely matched or surpassed by the amounts you may have to spend to tackle the health issues that you'll have. Common ailments such as fatigue, poor digestion, skin problems, etc. can be dealt with fairly easily. But when it comes to the more serious ones – such as stomach ulcers, diabetes, cardiac and liver problems, etc., you're can't get rid of them with a few pills and tonics. These are going to be life-long money drainers and will leech the life out of you, literally.

So, here's a lot of money that could have been saved, could have been used for something better like going on the holiday or getting your parents something extra special for a birthday.

It has been found that under 15% of adults below the age of 24 believe in eating fresh fruits and vegetables. They survive mainly on grain-based products such as bread and pizzas, and on meat. Let's not talk about unhealthy foods like fries and doughnuts, because I'm not sure under which food category I can even categorize them – they seem to have so little of grains and pulses! These items would definitely be more expensive than the humble greens, peas and carrots. So, this is something that applies to people who do cook food at home but tend to take the easy route and don't spend on the cheaper but healthier raw ingredients.

Most people do want to cook good food; they enjoy watching television shows like Masterchef and The Great British Bake Off. But because they don't realise how economical and healthy eating vegetables and grains can be, they just make wishes about cooking spectacular meals.

An average student's life means 3-4 nights of pizza and plenty of food that's bought on campus. He or she is spending roughly 100 pounds a week on food that includes some that are made at home. The majority of the expense is for readymade and takeaway meals, while there are meals that friends usually have together after college or to celebrate a mate's birthday. This age group also tends to over-indulge in the booze, so there's an easy 100 pounds more that you can add to their culinary expenses.

Companies like UberEats, Deliveroo, and Just Eat have a huge grip on the English market; the business is estimated to be worth 3.6 billion pounds. Even the local pubs that deliver food to your homes have seen a spike in their revenues. Although it accounts for just 4% of the total delivery food business, their service frequency has increased by 59%, while companies like Deliveroo have seen a 650% spike in the number of orders they receive! For those who thought that takeaway food is cheaper than eating at a restaurant – think again. Studies have found that a person who eats out and orders food regularly is making a miserly one pound saving if he switches over purely to takeaway orders. However, if you eat in speciality restaurants, then you are making a substantial saving by ordering takeaway food. An average meal in say a Thai or Indian restaurant would cost you about 13 pounds, while takeaways from the same places come up to 7-8 pounds.

So, what's the solution? Well, it's pretty obvious, isn't eat? Prepare meals at home and pack your lunch to college or work! Spend a little more in the grocery section of your mall than on the readymade food counters, and start planning a meal schedule for yourself. Plan a diet for yourself a week ahead, head to the nearest grocery store, pick up the things that you need, and get meal prepping. For those who have busy schedules, spend 3-4 hours on one of your days off and chop up fruits, vegetables, and meat that you can use over the coming week. You could either cook them partially, marinate them to be used in the next couple of days, make salads of the pieces, or refrigerate them raw to be cooked.

I was first inspired to do this by Joe Wickes from Lean in 15, it's a great book to get started and gives you a lot of recipes to get you going and you don't have to be good at cooking, it's so simple. This may not be for everyone and you may be happier with a sandwich if you are then good for you, you've just made your life a hell of a lot simpler. Generally, as humans, we are creatures of habit and as I explained earlier mid-week meals are just fuel they don't have to be Michellin starred delights that make you do a pirouette of joy with each mouthful. You need to be committed to eating good healthy fat burning food but not allow it to burn a hole in your pocket. I have a rhyme to help you remember; *Get clever with your dinner the night before.* Ok, it doesn't rhyme at all, but I hope you get the meaning.

To show you just how much we are spending, I have purchased a standard lunch of sandwich, crisps and drink from a lower and higher end outlet. Stripped them down to show you exactly what you're getting for your money. Yes, that's correct I've spent my hard-earned money to make sure you don't so after reading this you have to start implementing this otherwise it was all for nothing.

And guess what the results are in so let's take a look at the numbers and show you where those savings can be made.

High-End Outlet

Roast Chicken Salad Sandwich - £3.30

Red Leicester and Onion Crisps - £1.00

Bottle Of Water - £1.25

Total - £5.55

Lower End Outlet

Chicken Salad Roll – £2.70

Chedder and Onion Crisp - £0.80

Bottle of Water - £1.30

Total - £4.80

So, let's say you enjoy the finer things in life and you have the high-end option every day, that's a whopping £27.75 a week, £111 a month, £1443.00 in a year and over a five-year period £7215.00!!

Now after I had stripped the sandwiches down and weighed each piece I then made a sandwich using the same weights and then noted how much the lunch fuel would cost.

Roasted Chicken Sandwich A'la Briggs - £0.63

Crisps from Multipack (Branded) - £0.21

Water from the tap - £0.00

Total Cost £0.84

Astonished!? You bet your worn out dilapidated socks you are!

I did make one minor change though, I swapped the mayo for a full-fat diary butter, far healthier than sugary mayonnaise. Now I'll take the same paragraph I've just used to show you how much you were spending previously but change the figures to the newly revised figures GYAP figures.

So, let's say you enjoy the finer things in life and you have the high-end option every day, that's £4.20 a week, £16.80 a month, £218.40 in a year and over a five-year period £1092.00!!

So, over that period we have just put £6123.00 straight into your pocket.

And don't just think of the money you'll be saving think of the health benefits now you know exactly what's going into your sandwich or the sandwich that you prepare for your children.

I can already hear some of you screaming, Briggs I don't want the same thing every day I like variety but when I buy a mixture of fresh things they tend to go off before I use them.

Well don't worry kids I've got it sorted, I've made the mistakes so you don't have to, just think of me like a modern-day Mr Muscle. If its salad or sandwiches they all require the fillings so make sure you've got plenty to fill up with. If your struggling for inspiration on salad's or sandwich fillings but you go to a shop every day go in again take a photo of their different choices and copy that. If you're really into fun and games, why don't you take a photo and then pretend to pick from the shop? (if you do that you're pretty sad, to be honest). But if you get your kicks from pretending you're in a shop then crack on! The biggest hack for me is filling your shelves with a Hollywood catwalk of "stars in reasonably priced jars"! This stuff keeps for weeks and its fucking gorgeous if used properly, just think you've got olives, capers, red roasted pepper, gherkins beetroot an explosion of flavour at your fingertips. And don't forget your old friend Tin Diesel otherwise known as tuna, salmon, three bean salad and sweetcorn this stuff keeps for years so good to give you variety in your lunch and will also help out if the Zombie apocalypse comes! Winner winner homemade chicken dinner!!

You don't have to stick to the same food every day, be encouraged to mix it up a bit and try and stay seasonal so you could buy fresh seasonal produce and as the seasons change so will your lunch.

The biggest key to making this process a successful one is plan, plan, plan and plan. If you keep walking up and down the shopping isles looking for inspiration then all you'll do is spend £30 on things that you don't need and you'll still be hungry and you'll be skint.

So, to summarise, make time, get organised, plan what you're going to eat and give yourself a payrise.

Chapter 4

Cashing in on Cashback Points Make your money work for you!!

The next time you visit a giant retail store like Tesco and Nectar, be sure you are earning while you are spending? Confused? You're shortly about to be amazed with the power of spending money at the right stores. In the right way now Tesco does feature prevalently in this chapter again there are other options but if I wrote them all down this chapter would take up the whole book. Have a look into whichever supermarket you shop at as they all do similar deals.

The most popular multinational supermarket chain that has been operational since 1919, Tesco has largely been credited with encouraging shoppers to learn the value of using their club cards and credit cards for better deals each they spend using them. The culture earning rewards points or cashback each time you spend using your card has been nurtured by Tesco since 1995. Thanks to the smart moves made by the management team of Tesco, they were able to prevent American-based retail store chain Walmart eating into their profits. The main attraction with Tesco is that it's not just their club cards, but even their credit cards and bank accounts could yield you reward points that can actually be used to your benefit. And I'm not talking about shoddy deals offered by banks, wherein you need to enter your confidential details on some third-party site and use that as a payment gateway to get a discount or earn points which can only be used to buy services or commodities that are of no use to you.

Let's look at some of the benefits Tesco has for you:

1. For every pound that you spend in Tesco using the Clubcard, you earn a point. There are other ways of earning points, but we'll get to them later.

2. When you have accumulated at least 150 points, you become eligible to get vouchers via post or online that could be

used the next time you visit a Tesco store for some more shopping. And the best part – no restrictions on what you use the vouchers for. So you aren't forced to get a canned roast chicken or extra-large condoms, you know things that you know you won't be needing.

3. The points are reviewed on a quarterly basis, so you can expect to receive these vouchers once every three months. In case you cannot collect the minimum number of points, they can be carried forward to the next quarter. And don't worry about points getting lapsed, because the ones you earn are valid for a good 2 years after they've been added to your ever-expanding wallet.

4. So how much are these points in terms of money? 500 points equal 5 pounds, but their value can be increased if you use them to buy products or services that have a partnership with Tesco. So, for example, you want to book train tickets, meals or cinema tickets and you have enough points to be converted into the train fare, then you can login to the partner site and make the booking. Just

ensure you select the Tesco club card mode of payment, or ask for your earned points to be used as the currency. The 5 pounds value gets quadrupled to 20 pounds when they're used on partner sites.

5. Here's a great trick to get your Tesco points to last longer. If you have say 10 pounds' worth points left in your account and they are about to expire, but you don't want to spend them just yet as you know you'll need them in the next couple of months, then you simply need to spend a small fraction of the voucher money on Club Card Boost site (and not on any other site). There's no minimum amount that you can spend so you could make a 1-pound payment; the remaining amount gets added back to your account and you get new vouchers issued for them. These are of course valid for 2 long years!

6. Now, let's look at some of the non-expenses ways in which you can earn points and vouchers. Tesco awards you with points when you take part in certain surveys conducted by them when you

provide details of when your utilities are due each month or talk about the last Tesco shop that you' been to. Did you know that giving them a review could fetch you 25 pounds each month?! The number of points you can earn in this last manner is capped to 25 points, so you will need to continue this as a habit if you want to keep the points adding up.

7. Tesco also allows you to earn points if you use e-wallets that have a tie-up with them. All you need to do is save your credit/debit card details in the payment portal, and use them in conjunction with the purchases you make with Tesco. The points automatically get added to your points section, and new members also get free, welcome points when they start using the third-party website or when you sign up with Tesco.

8. The next big thing that is offered by Tesco is points earned when you use their credit cards. While a purchase of 1 pound registered on the Clubcard would yield you one point, you earn 2 points for every 4 pounds you spend using Tesco credit cards at Tesco stores. You earn 2

points when you use a Tesco credit card for at least 8 pounds in other stores. A single transaction at the stores should be worth at least 4 and 8 pounds respectively for you to be able to earn the 2 points. They are not calculated on a number of transactions adding up to 4 pounds eventually.

9. The important thing to remember when it comes to credit cards is that you ideally should be paying off all balances in full when you get your bill so you don't have to pay interest on the outstanding amount. The same policy when coupled with the rewards points make the credit card a very handy money adding tool in your arsenal. But again, be careful to pay it on time we will come to interest in the later chapters.

10. Lastly, Tesco has great tie-ups with companies and stores, and where the points are always valued more than what you paid to get them. So, for example, let's assume that you ought something from an online store at 5 pounds without redeeming any Tesco points. You are, in effect, having to pay the full price to

make the purchase. Instead, you could use your gathered points, find out what they are worth and the purchase points that are much less in value than the product price. So, the points for which you'd paid just 1 pound could be worth the whole 5 points, thanks to the liaison between Tesco and the online store company.

11. Some of the companies that have such deals with Tesco are Prezzo and Cafe Rouge, where you get up to 4 times the value of what you bought in the first place. So, this means points for which you spent 2.50 pounds are worth 10 pounds if you use them at such restaurants. Along the similar lines are cinema halls such as Odeon and Cineworld where points' value is increased three times, but only in certain areas. If you want to take out magazine subscriptions, then better check if they have any deals with Tesco like Marie Claire and Autocar do. Here, the value of the tickets is two times more than their actual price. Some of the other companies are:

a. Jewellery stores such as Goldmsiths – 3x value

b. Ticket booking sites such as RedSpottedHanky – 2x value

c. Hampton Court Palace and the London Zoo – 4x value

The main objective of using cards from Nectar or Tesco is that they reward you each time you use their services or shop in their stores, and these rewards can be put to really good use as and when your need arises. Purchases you made over the past 6 months at Tesco to buy your daily groceries could be sufficient to fund your next train ticket back home! It is important you keep track of the points you have, the vouchers you receive, and their expiration points. Calculate what is the maximum value you can get out of the vouchers and points that you have and put the points to use accordingly. For example, you have 10,000 points that can get you flight ticket to home and grocery supplies for the next month. The expenditure of the points or vouchers here becomes a very subjective matter. If you've not been to visit your parents for the past 2 years, then you need to book those train tickets more than you need groceries. But if you just been home and came back pretty recently, then you don't need to boom flight tickets and all the voucher you have can be used to stock your kitchen with grocery items.

Chapter 5

Getting Cautious with Cashback Websites

An interesting thing about word-of-mouth popularity is that the person making you, your company, or products famous is one who can sway people according to their preferences. Such people are known as charming or persuasive people. This is the basic principle based on which companies hire celebrities to promote their brand, although the celebrity may have never used their products or services, or may not even be particularly intelligent. So, what's in it for all? The company that has hired the celebrity can see a spike in their sales and earnings, and the person who became the "brand ambassador" is also rewarded for being able to send more paying customers in the direction of the seller company. It's a win-win situation for both parties involved.

Take this brand ambassador concept and apply it in the context of cashback websites. There are certain sites which have a number of ads posted by several companies. Because the ads are famous and have a wider reach (better than the company's influence area), the people who visit it are also more influenced by what they see on such sites. They may be tempted to click on the ads or hyperlinks of the sponsors. And then, they may be enticed to buy something that they didn't want to buy until then, or they may consider the cashback site itself to be a good lead to the main websites. So, what happens is the customer reaches the cashback site, get re-directed to the selling site, and then he/she deliberates on the purchases she wants to make on there. But there needs to be a trail of breadcrumbs that leads from the merchant site to the cashback site, else there's no moolah in it for you or for the cashback site. Let's see how this process goes in detail.

1. If you are looking to order a service or a product, don't go to the site of the sellers directly. Instead, look for a reliable cashback site which lists them on their partners' list.

2. Click on the link for these companies on such sites and you will be redirected to the merchant company's site, either via an external web page popping up, or the site itself being replaced by the merchant's website.

3. With the help of backlink technology, the merchant website can track that you, as a paying customer, were routed to their website via an intermediary site, and it is eligible for a small commission as a reward for advertising their link. This commission gets paid into the cashback website's account, of which a certain portion is added to your e-wallet of the cashback site. So, when you are signing up for an account on the cashback website, be sure to provide authentic details such as name, phone number, email and physical address, as required.

4. The money that gets accumulated in your e-wallet can then be transferred to your personal bank account using BACS payment, unless the cashback site gives you an option to use the money so collected for further shopping.

5. In order to get more internet footfall, leading merchants pay for affiliate links to appear in cashback websites. Some of these links as simply pa per click links, in which case the redirecting site simply gets a payment each time a customer clicks on anailiate link; these usually don't result in any cashbacks for the customers. So be sure to check whether the merchant site you are being redirected to is offering cashback upon using the cashback sites.

6. Some of the companies that offer cashbacks on cashback websites are Tesco, Argo, Debenhams (they offer 4% of the total product cost as cashback), Marks & Spencer (between 3 and 7% of products' cost), Currys (1-3%), Clarks (5%), Ensure car insurance (60 pounds per policy taken out), and Aviva home insurance (between 20 and 25 pounds per policy).

7. Some of the top cashback websites in the market currently are Quidco, Top Cashback.

8. Some of the payouts to the cashback websites and eventually to your personal account can take weeks, while some may even take up to a few months. So, it's important to keep a track of the purchases that you make, the cashback that you are guaranteed, and the final payout on a periodic basis. All cashback sites will allow you to visit your account registered on their site and check for the cashback you have accumulated.

Now there are a few rules associated with cashback websites you should keep in mind.

   a. The cashback amount that you are due to receive should be considered just as a bonus or perk, and not an assured payment like in the case of dividends on shares and insurance payouts. These are dependent on a number of factors, including any offers on-going with the merchant site, the period of settlement to the cashback website, and the agreement the cashback site has with you. It is quite possible that sometimes, the cashback websites themselves don't get any commission from the merchant site, in which case of course you aren't entitled to any. There are a number of disputes registered already, so don't make your purchases solely based on cashback offers.

b. Until the money reaches your bank account, the cashback that you've accumulated cannot be safely considered as yours. So, make it a habit to transfer cashbacks in your account regularly to your personal bank account, or utilise them for further transactions. The amounts that are usually paid out to the customers in the end are so small that they are difficult to pursue legally too, and there is little to zero protection that you can expect in such cases. So such purchases should be made solely on the basis of your research, discretion, and recommendations of friends who have safely used such websites.

c. Letting cashback accumulate in your cashback website e-wallet is a big no-no. Get into your account frequently, say every week at least, and check for any balances that can be transferred. If you are a frequent online shopper, then make it a habit to stop by the e-wallet every time you use the website and check for any such balances.

d. Finally, use your wisdom while making purchases and don't get lured into making purchases that you don't need or which are overpriced, just because you are getting an attractive cashback. Let's look at this point with an example. A buyer is looking to purchase a smartphone which is worth 520 pounds. The cashback site offers a 5% cashback, which means you are entitled to get 26 pounds as cashback. The irony is the actual cost of the phone is just 489 pounds on another website, so you are still paying 6 pounds more than you should have. Had you done your research correctly, you surely would have come across the lowest price, thus saving you some money a lot of hassle in waiting for the cashback to get credited and then transferring it to your own account.

e. In addition to offering you a cashback, some sites offer you a further discount if you register your credit/debit card details with them too, or make your purchases using specific banks' credit/debit cards. Remember that these deals are over and above the cashbacks being offered by the cashback site; so, if you hit the right combination you could save a lot of money.

f. Finally, remember that cashback sites have a strict policy when it comes to claiming your cashback amounts. Quidco, for example, allows you to access the amount only within 72 hours of it getting credited, while Topcashback allows you to claim it within 4 weeks of the cashback tracking.

g. the biggest rule of all don't get in to the habit of spending just because you get cashback, if you need to research it get cashback but don't go spending just because cashback is available it defeats the object. Prior to clicking that very addictive buy button ask yourself do I need it? Can I Afford it?

There are some people who have reported incomes of hundreds of pounds each month, thanks to smart shopping on cashback sites and using rewards and cashback credit/debit cards. You simply need to find the right cashback site and the merchant site combination, along with using precautionary measures such as installing an anti-virus application in your laptop or smartphone that you will be using to make your purchases, and activating anti-fraud checks with your banks to a certain extent.

Chapter 6

Cleaning Up the Direct Debit Closet

When you read this chapter heading the first thing that should come to more or less everyone is gym membership. At some point in your life I can guarantee we have all paid for the gym membership signed up with all good intentions of going to the gym 3-4 times a week and you never managed to go once not even for the induction. Come to think of it, some of our bank accounts are like behind-the-scenes closets that hide dark, dark skeletons, some of which even we are too guilty to face. How about those direct debits that you had got set up 5 years back but never bothered checking on since then? Finances can sometimes lead us to murky lands.

There were days when our parents would queue up in front of banks and stores to make their payments. Gone are those days, and standing orders and direct debits do make our lives much easier, no doubt about it. But what about the costs and risks associated with it? What about our inherent laziness coming to the fore when it comes to checking our bank statements and ensuring we are paying exactly what we were supposed to, and not inflated or unwanted fees? That's the pain area that needs to be constantly monitored to make direct debits exactly what they are – an economical convenience. Thanks to our lax checks, some companies misuse these conveniences in their favour and dupe us while we sit by and do nothing. Worse, we know nothing about these either.

Some of the top billers for whom we make use of direct debits most frequently are:

- Insurance companies – Roughly 5.5 million transactions are made per annum
- Mobile phone companies – 2.8 million approximately
- TV & Broadband Companies – 2.2 million approx
- Energy Agencies – 2 million approx

- Banks (Mortgage Payments) – 1.1 million approx
- Banks (Card Payments) – 1.1 million approx

Some of the other billers include the Council for tax and water supply, TV licensing companies, and bankers for loan EMIs. All of these, as you can see, are basic essentials that almost every household is reliant on, and hence we are talking about millions of direct debits. In fact, direct debits have become so popular that their volume has increased by a whopping 40% in the past decade, according to a survey done in 2013. It's been 4 years since then, so this number is likely to have gone further up.

So, what's the problem with direct debits, you may be wondering. Why do direct debits need any scrutiny to help you cut costs? Well, there are some very good reasons for you to do so.

1. There is a difference between standing instructions and direct debits, a big one. With direct debits, you are authorizing various merchants to debit your account of a certain sum on a periodic basis. The

problem is, the amount may vary if the biller deems it necessary. Let's take an example here. Say you are in the middle of a frantic meeting and you get a marketing call from your mobile company. They're offering you a great deal on this internet connection but you aren't interested in it. However, pressed for time and patience, you just mutter a lot of "yeses" to all the questions asked and lo, behold! You are the proud owner of a 4G internet connection that you'd never asked for. However, thanks to the direct debits you'd setup, the mobile company is authorised to debit payments from your bank account for a service that you never wanted. You don't even realise that you have a new service because we don't pay much attention to things such as mobile bills and tariff plans (negligence aboard!). So, your telephone company has authorised you to use a service that you probably never do, they increase your direct debit payments a little more than regular which you also fail to spot, and you end up shelling 40-50 pounds more over the course of a year! Had it been a standing instruction, you would have authorised your bank to make the payment, only after they get your confirmation, so the chances of you getting alerted to the higher payment are much higher with the latter method.

2. There are a number of affiliate companies and subscriptions that we tick in checkboxes while applying for services from banks and companies. Without us realising it, we may be subscribers to magazines related to the growth of the mushroom industry in Africa – such a big waste of money! Now it may seem like a small amount to you when you check your monthly subscription bill, but multiply that by 12 and you will surely feel the pinch.

3. In case of fraud, it is quite possible that your bills become larger and the money quietly leaves your account without making any blips. It is only when you decide to go over your accounts that you realise that you've paid more than you were supposed to, and the starts the process of raising a dispute and getting

the money settled back into your account.

4. The biggest problem with direct debits is that you pay a lot of unwanted bills without you realising it. There could be old subscriptions that still continue to be charged on your account, although you no longer use the services. Examples could be of magazine subscriptions, gym fees, donations to charitable organizations, etc. So if you're looking for a way to increasing your income, then you could start by first looking over your expenses and cutting out the unwanted expenses that have gradually been drained out of your account for a long time!

Chapter 7

Handling Debt Interests Like a Pro

As much as we want to, we cannot avoid debt forever in our lives. However, we should be trying everything to avoid and not go running in headfirst into a pay day loan. Some of these debts are for really large sums which stick to us for the majority of our lives. Property mortgages are the most common types of loans that require payments for a very long time, usually 20-30 years although creeping up to 30-40 years. Apart from mortgages, we also have personal loans, car loans, and credit card debts that need to be taken care of. So, what's common amongst all these types of debts? What should be paid special attention to when you plan to take any form of credit? Which factor should be considered in great detail to ensure you can pay your debt efficiently the answer to all these questions is APR!!

First of all ask yourself what is the difference between APR an interest?

Interest: money paid regularly at a particular rate for the use of money lent, or for delaying the repayment of a debt.

APR: abbreviation for Annual Percentage Rate: the rate at which someone who borrows money is charged, calculated over a period of twelve months.

So, in simple terms interest is the money you are charged for borrowing the money, APR is the full shooting match with admin charges, broker fee's etc. When considering a loan or credit card you must pay attention to the APR as that is what you will be paying on top of the money you have borrowed.

Unless you are a person who pays off his/her outstanding balance in full each month, you will have a substantial amount of interest to be paid on the balance. But unlike credit cards in which the interest could be avoided, the other types of debts don't have this facility. You must pay your bank a certain amount of interest for them lending you money or a facility. So, what's the problem with such debts? How can they be handled better to increase your savings and therefore your spendable or saveable income?

In the year 2016, credit card rates touched an all-time average high of 21.6% APR. Currently the Bank of England base rate is set to 0.5% so there is only one way it will go and give you a clue it's not down. Another important factor in terms of debts is your credit rating. Depending on how high your credit score is, you get suitable rated debts. The higher the score, lower would be the interest rate you have to shell out. For those who had poor scores and had to take debts at high interest rates – there's good news. You could opt for better interest rate deals when your credit rating is up a stable. Moral of this story is don't get in debt in the first place easier said than done I know, hence why the importance of managing your debt and finances efficiently is key to giving yourself a pay rise. As once you're in debt it's difficult to get out and its downward vicious circle.

According to a survey done in the first quarter of 2017, it has been confirmed that 7 out of 10 adults in UK have an average debt outstanding of £6,372. On a micro level, it has been found that the youth of today are the highest spenders and settle deeper into debt than the adults; 1 in 5 youth below the age of 30 owe £10,000 at any given time. Looking at debts region-wise, it has been found that Londoners have the deepest shade of red marking their ledgers, with debts totalling £10,244 outstanding per head. Unsecured debts for the entire nation stand at 240 billion pounds, and one in every three people in the country feel the need to rely on debt as a source of income on a monthly basis. It's tough to find people who are able to manage all their expenses based solely on their income without dipping into their savings or credit options. Some of the main factors which lead to the increase in debts are higher costs of living (with inflation at a high of 2.8%) and long-term debts that range for a minimum of two years.

The worst culprit for crippling people with debt are the people behind payday loans, they are a cancer to this country the very basic fundamentals of this poisonous scheme is toxic to your financial stability poison of this country I was watching the television recently when a loan for a payday advert young woman stood in front of her oven telling the camera how she was desperate for money as the cooker had broken and she 7 mouths to feed. If that was your situation it would be awful and you'd do anything to be able to feed your children however the APR was 1270% if you paid late, APR was 282% if you paid on time. This would mean if you had not paid anything off the loan and committed to pay it back within the month you would owe £1058.00 in interest plus the £1000 you already own. You should never entertain the thought of a payday loan. There are always other options the best one I can give you though is save so you don't even have to shop around for the best loan rates. How can you save when your out goings are larger than your income? Read chapter 1-6 and install those processes in to your life.

So, what are the options when it comes to making smart moves on debt-related interest rates?

1. Let's look at an example here. If you were to take out a loan of £7,500 at the rate of 3.3% APR (which is a very conservative

rate you're unlikely to get now-a-days!) and which lasts for a period of 5 years, then you end up paying £8,136.22 to your loan provider. That's over and above any fees associated with the loan you'd have to pay, such as processing fees, late payment fees, etc. And what do you have to show for this £636.22 you have paid to the bank? Worked out yet? Well its nothing I suppose you could sleep well knowing you have lined the pockets for a banker. Now, if you were to shop around for a balance transfer from a 1.5%. you would only be paying £112.50 in interest.

2. Consolidating a number of your debts into one large debt works cheaper because you have a standard rate of interest applicable to the whole amount, instead of paying a high rate on one amount and the medium-range APR on another. This does not mean go to a consolidation company they are cut from the same poison as pay day loans. All you need is an internet connection, a pencil and a calculator. Don't be afraid to call them either, get your top 3 from the net

then give them a call push to get that extra .01% off, after all its your money so take charge of it.

3. Switch to bankers who have 0% interest rate introductory offers and try and get this offer for a long period. This would help you pay off your debts without adding any interest on the outstanding amount while the debts are getting cleared. The better your credit score, the longer your introductory 0% rate period could stretch.

4. Usually, there are fees involved in switching from one bank to another, but this would be a one-time fee. Compare it with the savings that you'll be making over the period of the debt duration and make your decision.

Synopsis The Habit Of Spending

If you've reached this point, well done! You've purchased this life changing monologue, you've become more financially savvy with every page turned and if you've followed the instructions you have already reaped the benefits of this book before finishing it.

Most of the issues that have been noted have been through either financial unknowing or just the habit of spending. The time is now upon you to break that habit, improve your wealth and get financially savvy, you don't have to be obsessed with money but don't watch it flit away its better with you than with anyone else.

Good Luck!

Printed in Great Britain
by Amazon